I0821026

THE 1950s
THROUGH THE DECADES
Eureka!
BY SARA GREEN
LAKERS
21
Charlotte's Web
SONY
7 TRANSISTOR

Eureka! books turn real stories into unforgettable experiences. This nonfiction imprint sparks curiosity, encourages critical thinking, and engages middle-grade readers. *Eureka!* books empower young minds to explore the stories of the real world, one fascinating fact at a time. Unravel the power of knowledge and lifelong learning with *Eureka!*

This edition first published in 2026 by Bellwether Media, Inc.

No part of this publication may be reproduced in whole or in part without written permission of the publisher. For information regarding permission, write to Bellwether Media, Inc., Attention: Permissions Department, 3500 American Blvd W, Suite 150, Bloomington, MN 55431.

Library of Congress Cataloging-in-Publication Data

LC record for The 1950s available at: https://lccn.loc.gov/2025021825

Text copyright © 2026 by Bellwether Media, Inc. EUREKA! and associated logos are trademarks and/or registered trademarks of Bellwether Media, Inc. Bellwether Media is a division of FlutterBee Education Group.

Editor: Rebecca Sabelko Designer: Andrea Schneider

Printed in the United States of America, North Mankato, MN.

TABLE OF CONTENTS

WELCOME TO THE 1950s!

It is a Friday afternoon in 1955. A girl arrives home from school to find a souped-up Chevrolet Bel Air parked in the driveway. Hooray! Her eldest brother is visiting from college. He is going to spin records at the high school's **sock hop** that night. His collection of **45s** should keep the kids dancing for hours! The girl cannot wait until she is old enough to go to sock hops. Her brother promised to play "Rock Around the Clock" by Bill Haley & His Comets in her honor. It is her favorite song and one of the year's biggest hits!

The girl hums "Rock Around the Clock" as she dances into the kitchen to drop off her lunch box. Her mother looks up from peeling potatoes to say hello before checking on the meatloaf baking in the oven. The girl rushes to her room to change out of her school clothes. She grabs her roller skates for a quick spin around the neighborhood. After dinner, her family gathers in the living room to watch *The Adventures of Ozzie and Harriet* on television. This show is the bee's knees!

CHEVROLET BEL AIR

45

BILL HALEY & HIS COMETS

SOCK HOP

WHAT HAPPENED IN THE 1950s?

The 1950s were marked by growth, change, and conflict. The United States and the **Soviet Union** emerged from World War II as military superpowers. Tensions between the two countries and their allies were high during parts of the decade, fueled in part by the threat of **atomic weapons**. Their struggle, called the **Cold War**, would last from 1947 to 1991. Tensions also ran high in other parts of the world. The Korean War began in 1950 and would last for three years. Revolts in Kenya, Algeria, Egypt, and other countries aimed to end **colonialism**.

After World War II ended, the U.S. experienced an economic boom, maintaining its status as the world's richest country. This postwar prosperity allowed more people to buy homes, cars, and other expensive goods. The 1950s also saw the dawn of a new youth culture strengthened by a style of music called rock and roll. It would become one of the most influential musical **genres** of all time. The American Civil Rights Movement was also gaining strength. It sought to end racial **segregation** and **discrimination** against Black Americans across the country.

rock and roll legend Little Richard

HOW MUCH?

1 GALLON GAS
$0.27 (1950)
$0.31 (1959)

THE NEW YORK TIMES
(late city edition)
$0.05 (1950) | $0.07 (1959)

1 GALLON MILK
$0.83 (1950)
$1.01 (1959)

MOVIE TICKET
$0.46 (1950)
$0.68 (1959)

CANDY BAR
$0.05 (1950)
$0.05 (1959)

BOTTLE OF COKE
$0.05 (1950)
$0.05 (1959)

LOAF OF BREAD
$0.12 (1950)
$0.20 (1959)

HISTORY

UNITED STATES HISTORY

The U.S. was deep into the Cold War when the 1950s began. Atomic weapons had been created in the 1940s, but the 1950s witnessed the development of an even more powerful weapon of mass destruction called the hydrogen bomb. The U.S. and the Soviet Union began developing and testing hydrogen bombs, leading to widespread fear of a **nuclear war**.

The decade was also a time of new beginnings. The Civil Rights Movement began in the mid-1950s. Disneyland opened its gates on July 17, 1955. One million people visited the park in its first ten weeks! The National Aeronautics and Space Administration (NASA) began in 1958 to advance space exploration. The U.S. added two more stars to its flag when Alaska and Hawaii became states in 1959.

TESTING A HYDROGEN BOMB

CIVIL RIGHTS MOVEMENT PROTEST

OPENING DAY AT DISNEYLAND

MONTGOMERY BUS BOYCOTT

In 1955, a Black woman named Rosa Parks refused to give up her bus seat to a white man in Montgomery, Alabama. Parks was arrested, leading to massive protests led by Martin Luther King Jr. A majority of the city's Black residents boycotted the Montgomery bus system to protest segregation on public transportation. The boycott led to a 1956 Supreme Court decision declaring that Montgomery's segregation laws on buses were unconstitutional.

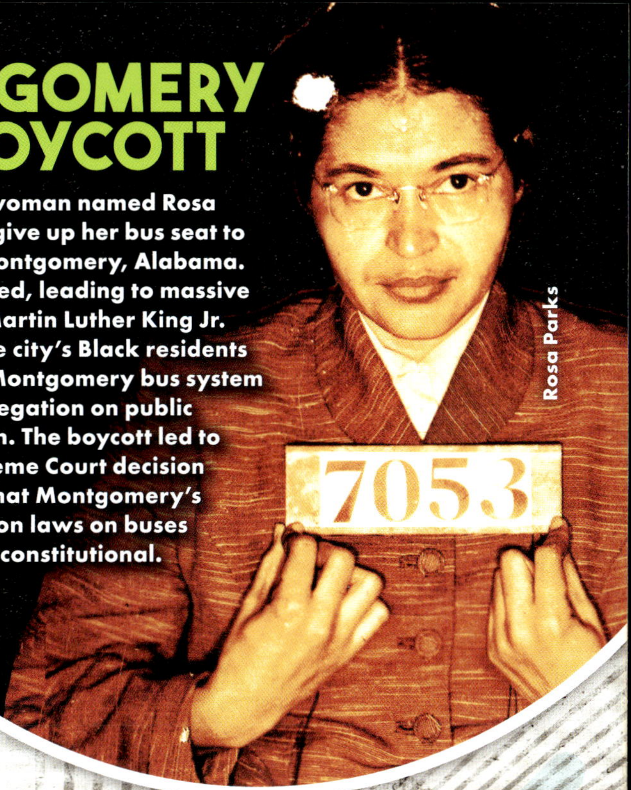

Rosa Parks

Senator Joseph McCarthy

RED SCARE

As the Cold War intensified, many people began to worry that communists were infiltrating U.S. society. This fear and paranoia became known as the Red Scare. Senator Joseph McCarthy contributed to the hysteria in the early 1950s by leading a campaign against alleged communists in the government and entertainment industries.

AMERICAN INDIAN URBAN RELOCATION

In 1952, the Bureau of Indian Affairs began a voluntary urban relocation program that pushed Native Americans to move from reservations to cities. Its goal was to assimilate Native Americans into mainstream society. However, many Native Americans faced challenges, including low-paying jobs, discrimination, and cultural isolation.

OPENING DAY

In April 1955, Ray Kroc opened the first McDonald's franchise in Des Plaines, Illinois. The menu offered nine items, including burgers, fries, and milkshakes. By 1958, McDonald's had sold 100 million burgers!

UNITED STATES POLITICS

The 1950s began with Harry Truman as U.S. President. Although Americans widely supported Truman during the 1940s, their support plunged due to the Korean War. Truman decided not to run for a third term. He would be the last president who could have served three terms. In 1951, the 22nd Amendment to the U.S. Constitution was approved. It states that a person cannot serve more than two terms as president.

President Dwight D. Eisenhower

ELECTION SHOWDOWN: 1952 PRESIDENTIAL ELECTION

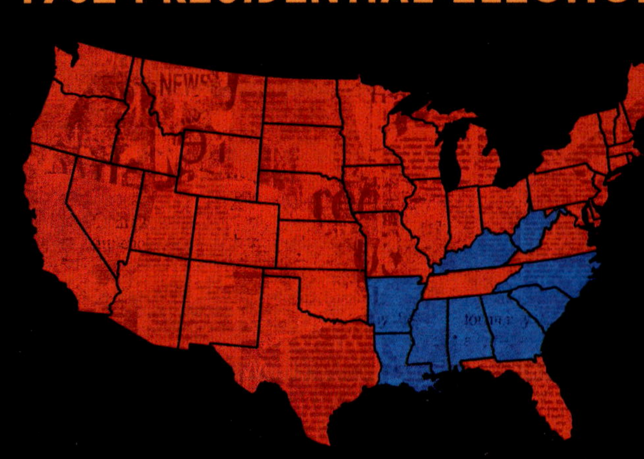

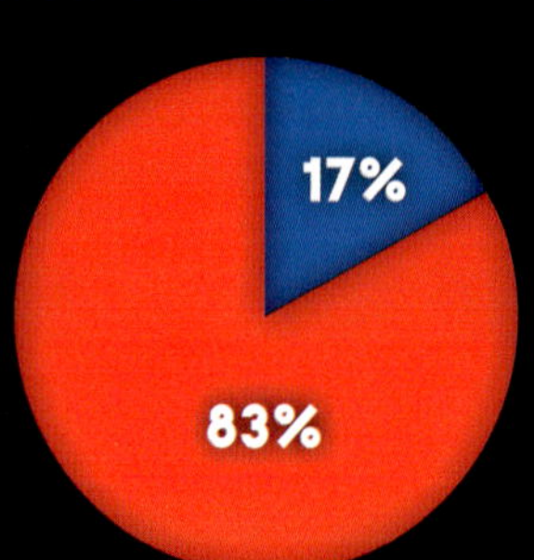

In 1952, former U.S. Army General Dwight D. Eisenhower was elected president. President Eisenhower, also known as Ike, was a likeable, moderate Republican and a World War II hero. Driven to create world peace, he negotiated an **armistice** in the Korean War and worked to lessen the tensions of the Cold War. Eisenhower also established the interstate highway system to better connect major cities. It led to the construction of more than 40,000 miles (64,374 kilometers) of highways. In 1956, President Eisenhower was reelected for a second term.

The decade also witnessed the growth of the Civil Rights Movement. In the 1954 landmark *Brown v. Board of Education* decision, the U.S. Supreme Court ruled that state laws that separated public schools for Black and white students were unconstitutional. This ruling set the stage for widespread desegregation. In 1957, Congress passed the Civil Rights Act. It was the first civil rights legislation since the 1800s and was aimed at protecting voting rights for Black Americans.

EISENHOWER CAMPAIGN EVENT

CLASSROOM AFTER DESEGREGATION IN 1954

EISENHOWER SIGNING THE CIVIL RIGHTS ACT

AFL-CIO MERGER

In 1955, the American Federation of Labor (AFL) and the Congress of Industrial Organizations (CIO) merged to form the AFL-CIO, becoming a powerful force in American labor and politics.

SPOTLIGHT ON:

BROWN V. BOARD OF EDUCATION

In the early 1950s, many parts of the U.S., especially the South, enforced the "separate but equal" system that the Supreme Court had declared legal in 1896. Black people were forced to use separate parks, restaurants, schools, and other public facilities. The National Association for the Advancement of Colored People (NAACP) set out to challenge the system. They asked Oliver Brown to try to enroll his daughter Linda in an all-white elementary school near their home in Topeka, Kansas.

"Equal Education For All"

–The Washington Post, May 19, 1954

MAKING HEADLINES

"High Court Outlaws Segregation in Schools"

–The Arizona Daily Star, May 18, 1954

"HIGH COURT BANS SCHOOL SEGREGATION; 9-TO-0 DECISION GRANTS TIME TO COMPLY"

–THE NEW YORK TIMES, MAY 18, 1954

After Linda was denied entry, Brown filed a **class-action lawsuit** against the Topeka Board of Education. He claimed that schools for Black children were not equal to schools for white children. The case went before the U.S. District Court in Kansas, but the court upheld the "separate but equal" system. The case was then appealed to the Supreme Court. Thurgood Marshall, a Black lawyer for the NAACP, argued that school segregation violated the 14th Amendment to the U.S. Constitution. It requires all U.S. citizens be treated the same, regardless of race. Marshall's argument was successful. In 1954, the U.S. Supreme Court ruled in a 9–0 decision that racial segregation in schools was unconstitutional. It ordered federal district courts to desegregate schools. However, many southern states refused to obey the order.

The struggle for school desegregation would continue for years. Still, the *Brown v. Board of Education* decision helped fuel the growing Civil Rights Movement in the U.S.

Linda Brown

WHO'S WHO?

THURGOOD MARSHALL

ROLE:
Civil Rights lawyer

KNOWN FOR:
Marshall used the courts to eliminate segregation and pursue racial justice, becoming the nation's first Black U.S. Supreme Court justice in 1967.

WORLD HISTORY

The 1950s ushered in a time of change around the world. Soviet dictator Joseph Stalin died in 1953 after decades of cruel leadership. Nikita Khrushchev soon rose to power. Khrushchev relaxed Stalin's harsh cultural policies during a period known as the "Khrushchev Thaw."

Numerous countries in Asia and Africa gained independence from European colonial rulers. Among them were Cambodia, Laos, Morocco, and Tunisia, which gained independence from France, and the Gold Coast, which was renamed Ghana after achieving independence from Britain. In 1954, Vietnam was divided into two countries: North Vietnam and South Vietnam. North Vietnam was led by the Vietnamese Communist Party, while the U.S. supported South Vietnam.

Important alliances also formed during the decade. The Warsaw Pact, formed in 1955, was a military alliance between the Soviet Union and seven Eastern European countries. A common market called the European Economic Community was established in Europe in 1957. It aimed to increase cooperation between European countries to create prosperity and promote peace.

NIKITA KHRUSHCHEV

SIGNING OF THE WARSAW PACT

MOROCCANS CELEBRATING THEIR INDEPENDENCE

WARSAW PACT

In 1955, West Germany became a military power by joining the North Atlantic Treaty Organization (NATO). In response, the Soviet Union formed the Warsaw Pact. Members pledged mutual military defense of any member. The pact strengthened the Soviet Union's control over its member states. In a show of power, the Soviet Union used Warsaw Pact troops to crush an anti-Soviet uprising in Hungary in 1956, dashing any hopes of democracy in Eastern Europe at the time.

THE CUBAN REVOLUTION

In 1952, an anti-communist dictator named Fulgencio Batista seized power in Cuba. An armed revolt led by Fidel Castro in 1953 failed, but it signaled the start of the Cuban Revolution. After years of civil war, revolutionaries finally drove Batista out of Cuba in 1959. Before long, Castro developed ties with the Soviet Union and implemented a communist government. Castro would go on to lead Cuba until 2008.

Fidel Castro

British troops leaving the Suez Canal

SUEZ CRISIS

Before 1956, a British-French company managed Egypt's Suez Canal. Egyptian President Gamal Abdel Nasser took control of the important trade route in 1956. His announcement was a push toward decreasing British and French political influence in Egypt. Nasser's action led to a military invasion by Israel, France, and Britain. The United Nations (UN) forced these countries to withdraw from Egypt, averting a potential nuclear war.

SPACE RACE

In 1957, the Soviet Union launched Sputnik 1, the first artificial satellite. This event kickstarted the space race between the U.S. and the Soviet Union.

Sputnik 1

SPOTLIGHT ON:

THE KOREAN WAR

By the end of World War II, the country of Korea had been divided at the 38th parallel line. North Korea was a communist state backed by the Soviet Union. The U.S. supported South Korea. On June 25, 1950, North Korean forces invaded South Korea in a surprise attack and soon took over the South Korean capital of Seoul. It appeared that South Korea would be easily defeated. The U.S. quickly responded. On June 27, President Truman ordered U.S. forces to South Korea without officially declaring war. The UN agreed to assist the U.S. in the conflict. It sent forces from Australia, France, and other member countries. U.S. General Douglas MacArthur led UN forces. They were able to push North Korea back until October 19, when China joined North Korea after UN forces crossed the 38th parallel. Fighting escalated. Attempts at a peace negotiation in 1951 failed because the two sides could not agree on how their prisoners of war should be treated.

MAKING HEADLINES

"NORTH KOREANS INVADE SOUTH KOREA"

—*NEW YORK HERALD TRIBUNE*, JUNE 26, 1950

KOREAN WAR VETERANS MEMORIAL

The Korean War Veterans Memorial in Washington, D.C., honors the people who served in the Korean War. It features 19 statues of military personnel in action, a mural wall, the Pool of Remembrance, and the Wall of Remembrance.

KOREAN WAR VETERANS MEMORIAL

On July 27, 1953, leaders signed an armistice. It drew a new border between North Korea and South Korea. However, no formal peace treaty was ever signed. Nobody knows for sure how many people died in the war, but it is thought that the number could be as high as 4 million. Today, more than 7,500 Americans are still missing in action, and the two Koreas remain divided.

"KOREAN WAR IS ENDED IN TRUCE 'MUST NOT RELAX,' IKE WARNS"

—*THE CINCINNATI ENQUIRER*, JULY 27, 1953

"Capture of Seoul Claimed By Reds"

–*The San Francisco Chronicle*, June 28, 1950

WHO'S WHO?

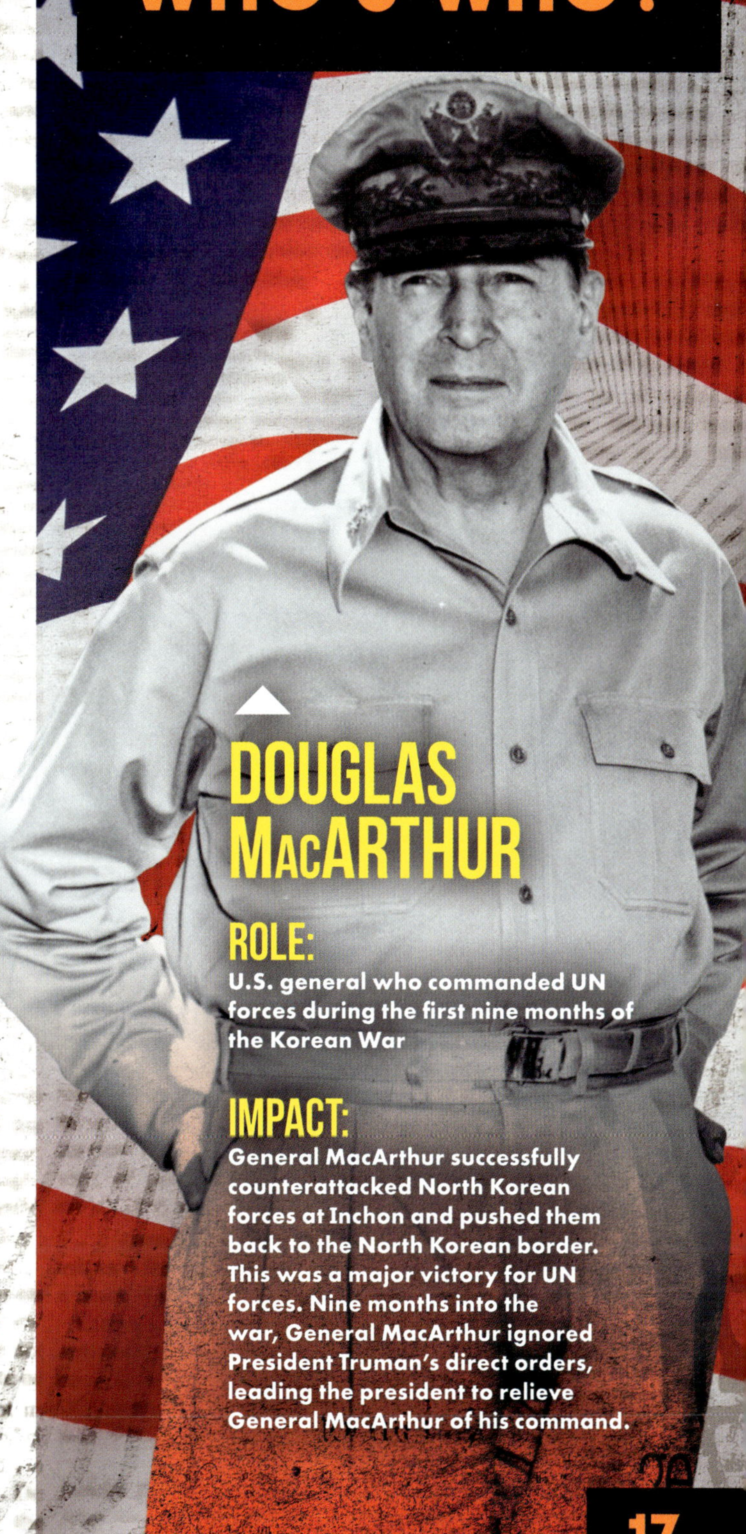

DOUGLAS MACARTHUR

ROLE:
U.S. general who commanded UN forces during the first nine months of the Korean War

IMPACT:
General MacArthur successfully counterattacked North Korean forces at Inchon and pushed them back to the North Korean border. This was a major victory for UN forces. Nine months into the war, General MacArthur ignored President Truman's direct orders, leading the president to relieve General MacArthur of his command.

SOCIAL CHANGES

The American Dream of the 1950s included a family, a stable job, a home in the suburbs, and a car. The term "nuclear family" became widely used to describe an ideal family unit consisting of a straight married couple and children. Husbands worked outside the home and wives were homemakers. These roles were reinforced on television, in movies, and in magazines.

Despite its promises, the American Dream remained out of reach for many people. Discrimination and segregation prevented people of color from achieving the same level of economic success as white people. A growing number of women felt unfulfilled by traditional gender roles and the expectation of being homemakers. Many had joined the workforce during World War II and chose to keep their jobs despite being criticized.

The **LGBTQ+** community faced major barriers. People in the community were seen as morally corrupt, mentally ill, or dangerous to society. Most LGBTQ+ people had to hide their identities to avoid losing their jobs, family, and social standing. Many entered into traditional straight marriages to hide their true identities.

1950s "NUCLEAR FAMILY"

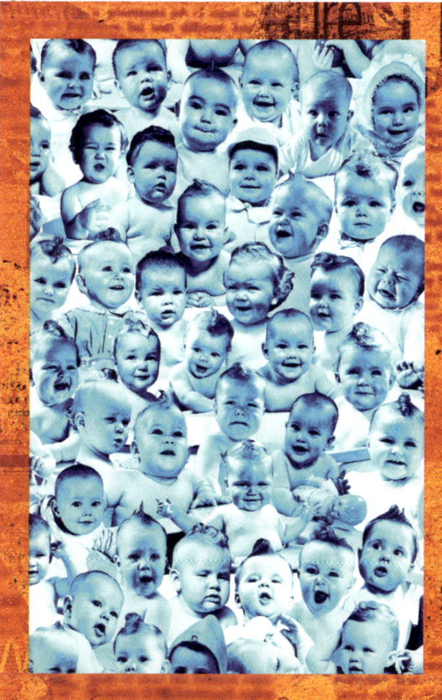

BABY BOOM

There was a large increase in the birth rate after World War II. The generation of Americans born between 1946 and 1964 became known as "baby boomers."

WOMEN IN THE WORKFORCE IN 1952

1950s SUBURB

SCIENCE AND TECHNOLOGY

TECHNOLOGY

The 1950s were a time of major scientific and technological advances. U.S. scientists first tested a hydrogen bomb, or H-bomb, in 1952. The H-bomb is a thousand times more powerful than the atomic bombs dropped on Japan during World War II. The H-bomb was dropped on an uninhabited island in the Pacific Ocean. The explosion vaporized the island and destroyed life on nearby islands. It also created serious health concerns for people in the surrounding area.

The first commercial flight service on a jet-powered passenger aircraft took to the sky in 1952 with 36 passengers on board. The jet was called the *Comet*. It was designed and made in the United Kingdom. In 1958, the Boeing 707 began regular air service with Pan American Airlines. This aircraft is often credited with ushering in the jet age. Within a few years, air travel surpassed rail and sea travel in popularity.

HOVERCRAFT

WHAT IS IT?:

A vehicle that glides above land, water, or ice on a cushion of air created by fans

INVENTOR:

Sir Christopher Sydney Cockerell

YEAR INVENTED:

1955

EFFECT ON DAILY LIFE:

The hovercraft was used to ferry people and automobiles across the English Channel for 40 years.

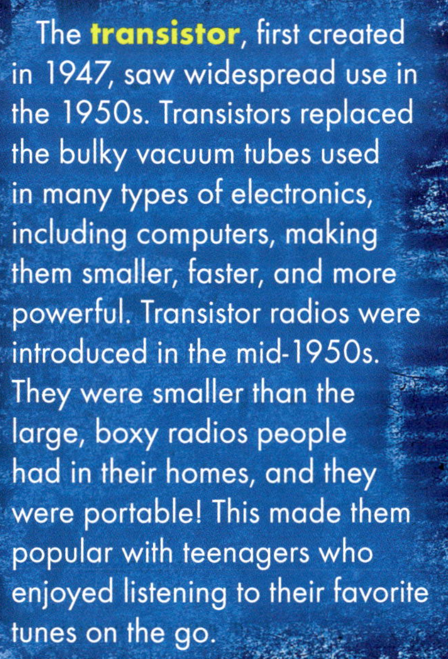

The **transistor**, first created in 1947, saw widespread use in the 1950s. Transistors replaced the bulky vacuum tubes used in many types of electronics, including computers, making them smaller, faster, and more powerful. Transistor radios were introduced in the mid-1950s. They were smaller than the large, boxy radios people had in their homes, and they were portable! This made them popular with teenagers who enjoyed listening to their favorite tunes on the go.

INSIDE A BOEING 707 IN 1958

cloud made from the first H-bomb in 1952

CROSS-COUNTRY CONNECTION

On November 10, 1951, the first coast-to-coast direct dial phone call was placed. The mayor of Englewood, New Jersey, called the mayor of Alameda, California. It took 18 seconds for the call to connect!

MEDICAL DISCOVERIES

The 1950s also saw major breakthroughs in medicine and biology. In 1953, Dr. John H. Gibbon Jr. successfully used a heart-lung machine during an operation for the first time. The machine takes over for the heart and lungs temporarily. This allows surgeons to perform surgeries on the heart and blood vessels while the heart is stopped. In 1954, Dr. Joseph Murray performed the first successful human kidney transplant on identical twins. His groundbreaking work paved the way for transplants of other organs, too. Today, thousands of people undergo organ transplants each year to improve and often extend their lives.

In 1953, James Watson and Francis Crick discovered the structure of **DNA**. It has a structure like a twisted ladder and splits in half when a cell divides. This gives DNA the ability to pass along precise biological instructions. Their breakthrough laid the foundation for modern **genetics**.

structure of a section of DNA

In 1955, the results of Dr. Jonas Salk's vaccine against a crippling disease called poliomyelitis, or polio, proved to be effective. Within a few years, the number of cases dropped from thousands to just a handful in the U.S. The 1950s also saw the introduction of several new **antibiotics** such as tetracycline and erythromycin to treat bacterial infections. Some of these infections were once incurable and deadly. Widespread availability of vaccines and antibiotics led to a huge decrease in mortality rates and helped raise life expectancy around the world.

ROSALIND FRANKLIN

Scientist Rosalind Franklin played a key role in Watson and Crick's discovery of the structure of DNA. Her X-ray images revealed crucial information that Watson and Crick used to build their DNA model.

HEART-LUNG MACHINE

JAMES WATSON AND FRANCIS CRICK

ILLUSTRATION OF THE POLIO VIRUS

DAILY LIFE

LIFE IN THE '50s

The 1950s are often viewed with **nostalgia**, especially by middle-class white Americans. Jobs were plentiful and incomes grew. People could afford to buy cars, a necessity for those living in the expanding suburbs. Car models such as the Ford Thunderbird and the Chevrolet Bel Air became status symbols. Sales of televisions, furniture, and appliances also skyrocketed.

Before the 1950s, many kids had to start working at a young age to help provide for their families. The rapid advancement of the middle class in the 1950s changed that. Kids had more time to be kids! Suburban neighborhoods became playgrounds where kids could roller-skate and ride bikes with their friends. The rise of youth culture allowed teenagers to develop their own identity apart from their parents. They expressed themselves through music, fashion, and entertainment. Many parents disapproved of teen culture and viewed teens as rebellious.

For people of color, however, the 1950s were challenging. Many faced employment and educational discrimination. The practice of **redlining** made home ownership very difficult for Black people. In the South, Jim Crow laws enforced racial segregation in public places.

FORD THUNDERBIRD

TEENAGERS IN 1957

IN THE BANK

The annual average U.S. salary in the 1950s was $3,210. That equates to around $41,700 today.

1950s SLANG

a car with increased power

Cruisin' for a bruisin'

looking for trouble

something or someone who is admired

to have an easy life

Radioactive

popular

GIVE ME A BELL

call me

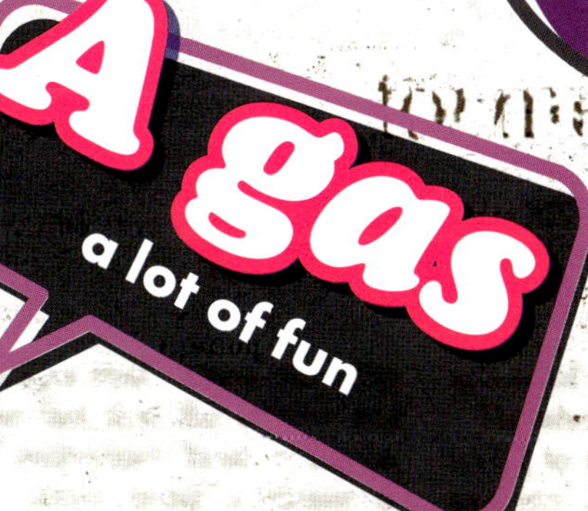

a lot of fun

Hipster

someone who is up-to-date on the latest counterculture trends

Cookin'

doing something well

money

FASHION TRENDS

Most people wore the same few styles before the 1950s. However, increased buying power and consumerism during the 1950s ignited the fashion scene. People began experimenting with new colors, styles, and looks. Full skirts called poodle skirts were popular, especially among teen girls. They featured designs, often a poodle, sewn near the hems. Many girls wore stiff garments under the skirts to add extra volume.

Women who preferred a more streamlined look wore pencil skirts for both casual and formal occasions. Pants were another popular trend for women, especially slim cigarette pants and capri pants.

James Dean

CAP CRAZE

A coonskin cap worn by Davy Crockett, a character featured on Walt Disney's weekly television show *Disneyland*, began a kids' fashion craze. An average of 5,000 coonskin caps were sold daily at the height of their popularity in the 1950s.

Teen boys often copied the styles of movie stars and rock and roll idols. Elvis Presley, James Dean, and Marlon Brando made jeans, white T-shirts, and leather jackets a huge trend! Many men opted for the Ivy League look, with its sweater vests, Oxford shirts, and tweed sports coats. Men could often be found relaxing in Hawaiian-style shirts.

The 1950s are also remembered for new hair trends. The poodle cut, the bouffant, the beehive, and the pixie were popular hairstyles for women. Men had many hairstyle options, too. Some, such as the ducktail and pompadour, were popularized by Elvis Presley, James Dean, and other stars of the decade. The flattop was also a popular men's haircut.

bouffant hairstyle

POODLE SKIRT

IVY LEAGUE STYLE

ELVIS PRESLEY WITH A POMPADOUR HAIRSTYLE

PRODUCTS AND TOYS

Toy sales surged in the 1950s due to the economic boom and the growth of commercial advertising on television. Many of the decade's most popular toys were made of plastic, which had become increasingly available after World War II. Plastic was ideal for making cheap, colorful, and long-lasting toys!

BARBIE

Barbie was launched by Mattel in 1959. The doll was a smash hit! Soon, different versions of Barbie were released. Each had different clothing and accessories. Over time, more than a billion Barbie dolls would sell around the world, making Barbie the most successful doll in history.

MATCHBOX CARS

Matchbox Cars were introduced in 1953. They got their name because they were the size of a matchbox! Early models included a race car, a cement mixer, and a double-decker bus. Their detailed designs and affordable prices made them hugely popular.

FISHER-PRICE LITTLE PEOPLE

Fisher-Price started its Little People toy brand in 1950 with the Looky Fire Truck and three small, round-headed firefighters. Over time, the Little People line would grow to include a variety of playsets, including houses, farms, and vehicles. Since the brand's launch, more than 2 billion Little People figures have been sold in more than 60 countries!

HULA HOOP

The Hula Hoop, introduced by Wham-O in 1958, became a huge fad. More than 20 million Hula Hoops were sold within the first few months of sales. Both children and adults enjoyed spinning the simple plastic hoops around their waists!

MR. POTATO HEAD

Mr. Potato Head debuted in 1952. The kit included plastic eyes, noses, mouths, hats, and other accessories. Kids pinned the pieces on real potatoes to make funny faces. Mr. Potato Head earned $4 million in sales in just a few months. Mrs. Potato Head was introduced in 1953.

LEGO BRICKS

The LEGO toy company introduced the interlocking LEGO brick in the 1950s. It quickly became the company's signature product. LEGO would go on to launch building sets, theme parks, and minifigures. People of all ages enjoy creating with LEGO!

PLAY-DOH

Play-Doh started in the 1930s as a wallpaper cleaner that removed soot from walls created from coal heating. The putty became a popular children's modeling toy in 1956 after gas and oil heating grew more common. Sales of Play-Doh skyrocketed after it was advertised on the popular children's television show *Captain Kangaroo*.

ARTS AND ENTERTAINMENT

PUBLICATIONS

Authors in the 1950s were influenced by a variety of factors. The Cold War contributed to the rise of spy novels, such as Ian Fleming's James Bond series. Authors like Ralph Ellison and James Baldwin addressed the injustice and social change that spurred the Civil Rights Movement. The rise of the Beat Generation led to books that explored themes of rebellion and personal freedom.

Charles Schulz's first *Peanuts* comic strip debuted in 1950. It introduced readers to Charlie Brown, Snoopy, and the rest of the Peanuts gang. Dr. Seuss gave readers *The Cat in the Hat*, *Horton Hears a Who*, and *How the Grinch Stole Christmas*. These books would become timeless delights for children around the world.

READING REC

TITLE:
HENRY HUGGINS

AUTHOR:
Beverly Cleary

YEAR PUBLISHED:
1950

SUMMARY:
The boring life of third-grader Henry Huggins turns topsy-turvy after he rescues a stray dog he names Ribsy.

THE CATCHER IN THE RYE

Published in 1951, J.D. Salinger's novel about teenager Holden Caulfield became an instant classic. Readers often identify with its themes of teenage angst and rebellion. It remains a staple of American literature today.

CHILDREN'S CLASSICS

Dozens of classic children's novels were published during the 1950s. Among them were *Charlotte's Web* by E.B. White, *The Lion, the Witch, and the Wardrobe* by C.S. Lewis, and *Beezus and Ramona* by Beverly Cleary. Children's literature introduced readers to some of the most beloved characters of all time!

MAGAZINES

Magazines were a popular source of entertainment for people of all ages in the 1950s. Some, such as *TV Guide* and *Sports Illustrated*, became staples in many households. *Popular Electronics* was aimed at do-it-yourself electronics enthusiasts. The puzzles, stories, and activities in *Highlights for Children* delighted younger children, while *Mad* magazine's biting humor resonated with teens.

THE DIARY OF A YOUNG GIRL

The Diary of a Young Girl by Anne Frank was published in English in 1952. It gives readers a firsthand look at the daily life and emotions of a young teen forced to hide with her family during the Holocaust. Anne's story teaches readers about the horrors of the Holocaust, while promoting tolerance, understanding, and hope.

Anne Frank

MOVIES

The film industry faced setbacks in the 1950s due to labor conflicts, the popularity of television, and declining ticket sales. But the industry found creative ways to combat these challenges. Filmmakers used new techniques such as color film, **stereophonic sound**, widescreen formats, and 3D to make movies more spectacular. This led to the rise of blockbuster films. These grand epics enchanted audiences with their sweeping tales of adventure and romance.

Filmmakers found additional ways to attract audiences to theaters. They improved their storytelling and made films that targeted teen audiences. Some used gimmicks such as prize giveaways, scented screenings, and seats rigged with electric buzzers!

DRIVE-IN THEATERS

Although they had been around since the 1930s, drive-in theaters took off in the 1950s. There were more than 4,000 drive-ins around the country by 1958. People enjoyed watching movies on gigantic outdoor screens from the comfort of their cars. Drive-in theaters were especially popular with teens and families with children.

AT THE BOX OFFICE

TOP-GROSSING FILMS OF THE 1950s

- ***Lady and the Tramp*** **(1955)**
- ***Cinderella*** **(1950)**
- ***Peter Pan*** **(1953)**
- ***Ben-Hur*** **(1959)**
- ***The Ten Commandments*** **(1956)**
- ***Sleeping Beauty*** **(1959)**
- ***Some Like It Hot*** **(1959)**
- ***Around the World in 80 Days*** **(1956)**
- ***This Is Cinerama*** **(1952)**
- ***Rear Window*** **(1954)**

Ben-Hur

20,000 LEAGUES UNDER THE SEA

This 1954 live-action Disney adventure film is based on the novel by Jules Verne. It stars James Mason as Captain Nemo and Kirk Douglas as Ned Land. The film was praised for its imaginative storytelling and special effects. Its giant squid battle is among the film's most famous scenes!

TEENS AT THE MOVIES

Teen culture had a major influence on filmmakers in the 1950s. Movies such as *Rebel Without a Cause* and *Blackboard Jungle* focused on youth rebellion and the struggles of growing up. Horror and creature movies such as *Godzilla* and *The Blob* also drew large teen audiences.

Godzilla

SINGIN' IN THE RAIN

The musical comedy *Singin' in the Rain* came out in 1952. It stars Gene Kelly, Debbie Reynolds, and Donald O'Connor. The film is set in Hollywood during the transition from silent films to talkies, or films with sound. It is known for its memorable song and dance numbers, especially the title song.

ANIMATED DISNEY CLASSICS

Disney released several animated films in the 1950s that are now considered classics. *Cinderella* and *Peter Pan* were huge box office successes. *Lady and the Tramp* was the highest-grossing movie of 1955! *Alice in Wonderland* and *Sleeping Beauty* also gained popularity over time.

Lady and the Tramp

BEN-HUR

The historical drama *Ben-Hur* hit theaters in 1959. This blockbuster movie starring Charlton Heston was a massive hit. It won 11 Academy Awards, including Best Picture. Its spectacular chariot race is one of the most famous action sequences in film history!

TELEVISION

The 1950s saw a rapid growth in television ownership. In 1949, around 1 million American homes had TV sets. That number increased to 50 million by 1959!

Television impacted society in many ways. Shows like *Father Knows Best* and *Leave It to Beaver* influenced people's ideas of what American family life should look like. Advertising became a powerful tool for shaping people's preferences. Televised news coverage brought the world into people's homes in ways that newspapers and radios could not. This changed the way people saw the U.S. and the world. Videotape technology changed how television was produced. Programming shifted from mainly live to recorded production.

U.S. Marshal Matt Dillon from *Gunsmoke*

GUNSMOKE

The western series *Gunsmoke* debuted in 1955. It aired for 20 seasons, becoming one of television's longest-running primetime shows. The series revolves around U.S. Marshal Matt Dillon, who is responsible for maintaining law and order in the frontier town of Dodge City, Kansas.

Father Knows Best

1959 TV set

quiz show *Twenty-One*

QUIZ SHOW SCANDALS

Quiz shows were extremely popular in the 1950s. However, a series of scandals revealed that some of the most popular quiz shows were rigged. Producers were secretly giving answers to favored contestants. Viewers were shocked, and many lost trust in quiz shows. The scandals prompted congressional investigations that led to changes in television game show regulations.

AMERICAN BANDSTAND

American Bandstand **was a popular dance show that debuted in 1952. It featured teenagers dancing to the latest hits and live performances by popular artists. The show played a huge role in promoting rock and roll music. It introduced audiences to many artists who would become famous in coming decades, including Prince, The Jackson 5, and Cher.**

American Bandstand

Lucille Ball from *I Love Lucy*

I LIKE IKE

Walt Disney Studios created an animated commercial called "I Like Ike" for Dwight D. Eisenhower's 1952 presidential campaign. It was the first political campaign ad to air on television. It helped Eisenhower win the election.

I LOVE LUCY

I Love Lucy, a sitcom starring Lucille Ball and Desi Arnaz, debuted in 1951. It quickly became television's number one comedy. *I Love Lucy* was one of the first shows with a female lead and a co-star from an ethnic minority group. The show was groundbreaking for its use of a three-camera setup and a live audience.

MUSIC

The birth of rock and roll dominated the 1950s music scene. The genre was influenced by jazz, blues, country, and gospel music. Artists such as Elvis Presley, Bill Haley, and Chuck Berry topped the charts and left a lasting impact on the music industry. Rock and roll bridged racial divides by creating a shared culture among Black and white teenagers. Many adults, on the other hand, found rock music to be vulgar. They feared it would turn teens into delinquents!

The 1950s also saw major innovations in musical instruments. **Synthesizers** and the rising popularity of basses and electric guitars gave musicians the tools to create exciting new sounds!

FENDER STRATOCASTER

Fender launched the Stratocaster electric guitar in 1954. Its sleek body, pitch-changing system, and wide range of tones offered musicians more options and greater comfort than earlier guitars.

1950s PLAYLIST

- ***Get Happy***
  Judy Garland (1950)
- ***Mona Lisa***
  Nat King Cole (1950)
- ***Come On-a My House***
  Rosemary Clooney (1951)
- ***Rock Around the Clock***
  Bill Haley & His Comets (1954)
- ***Tutti Frutti***
  Little Richard (1955)
- ***Don't Be Cruel***
  Elvis Presley (1956)
- ***Blueberry Hill***
  Fats Domino (1956)
- ***Bye Bye Love***
  The Everly Brothers (1957)
- ***Walkin' After Midnight***
  Patsy Cline (1957)
- ***La Bamba***
  Ritchie Valens (1958)

AN AMERICAN DIVA

Marian Anderson became the first Black soloist to sing at New York's Metropolitan Opera House on January 7, 1955.

Elvis Presley

ELVIS PRESLEY

Elvis Presley is often referred to as the "King of Rock and Roll." His electrifying performances and groundbreaking hits made him an international sensation. He had 114 Top 40 hits, including "Heartbreak Hotel," "Hound Dog," "Jailhouse Rock," and "Love Me Tender." Elvis ranks among the world's most influential and best-selling artists in popular music history!

CHUCK BERRY

Chuck Berry was a pioneer of rock and roll. His innovative guitar playing and clever lyrics made him one of the most defining musicians of the 1950s. Hits like "Johnny B. Goode," "Maybellene," and "Roll Over Beethoven" united music lovers of different races. The songs topped the charts and became classics that defined a generation.

Chuck Berry

DANCE CRAZES

Many fun dance crazes took off in the 1950s. The Hand Jive involves complicated hand and arm movements performed while sitting or standing. Dancers jump forward, backward, and sideways doing the Bunny Hop. The Stroll is a group dance where people face each other in lines. Couples pair up and take turns slowly dancing down the center aisle together.

AM RADIO

AM radio was the dominant form of broadcast radio in the 1950s. It provided a wide range of music, news, and entertainment programming. Popular music shows and DJs played the latest hits on AM radio, making it a primary source of music for many people.

JUKEBOXES →

Jukeboxes are coin-operated machines that play selected records. Jukeboxes were a popular way for people to listen to their favorite songs in public in the 1950s, especially in diners and dance halls. Although jukeboxes had been around for decades, they reached the peak of their popularity in the 1950s. They often had flashy features, including chrome finishes, bubble tubes, and tailfins!

U.S. SPORTS

Spectator sports surged in popularity with the spread of television. Major League Baseball (MLB) remained America's national pastime. New York was home to the decade's three top teams: the Yankees, the Dodgers, and the Giants. The Yankees dominated the sport with six World Series wins during the decade. Larger-than-life baseball champions Mickey Mantle and Willy Mays captivated fans across the country.

The National Basketball Association (NBA) and the National Football League (NFL) built larger fan bases. Boxing legends Rocky Mariano and Sugar Ray Robinson took the ring by storm.

BREAKING BARRIERS

In 1953, pilot Jacqueline Cochran became the first woman to break the sound barrier. She flew a jet over Edwards Air Force Base at an average speed of 652 miles (1,049 kilometers) per hour.

MVP

NAME:
DICK BUTTON

SPORT:
Figure Skating

NATIONALITY:
American

YEARS ACTIVE:
Late 1940s to the early 1950s

KNOWN FOR:
Dick Button won two Olympic gold medals, the first in 1948 and the second in 1952. In 1951, Button became the first figure skater to complete a double axel. He also landed the first triple loop in the 1952 Olympics.

1958 NFL CHAMPIONSHIP GAME

The 1958 NFL Championship Game is widely known as "The Greatest Game Ever Played." The Baltimore Colts defeated the New York Giants 23–17 in the first playoff game to end in sudden-death overtime. This exciting game brought new fans to the NFL!

MLB CHAMPS

Mickey Mantle was a star slugger and center fielder for the Yankees. His speed and powerful switch-hitting made him a star. Willy Mays was a center fielder for the Giants before finishing his career with the Mets. Mays was known for his skills on both offense and defense. Both players were inducted into the National Baseball Hall of Fame in the 1970s.

BEN HOGAN

Ben Hogan was one of the greatest golfers of all time. He overcame a near-fatal car accident in 1949 to win multiple major championships in the 1950s. These included the Masters Tournament, the British Open, and the U.S. Open. Over the course of his career, Hogan won more than 60 professional golf tournaments.

GEORGE MIKAN

George Mikan played center for the Minneapolis Lakers. He was the NBA's first dominant "big man" and led the Lakers to multiple championships in the 1950s. *Associated Press* named him the greatest basketball player in the first half of the 20th century. Today, Mikan is considered one of the pioneers of professional basketball.

Althea Gibson

ALTHEA GIBSON

In 1950, Althea Gibson became the first Black woman to compete in a national tennis tournament. Gibson won 11 championships between 1956 and 1958, including the 1956 French Open, the 1957 and 1958 Wimbledon, and the 1957 and 1958 U.S. Nationals. Gibson was named the *Associated Press* Female Athlete of the Year in 1957 and 1958.

GLOBAL SPORTS

Athletes across the globe performed amazing feats during the 1950s. American Florence Chadwick broke world records for swimming the English Channel. She was also the first woman to swim the Catalina Channel, breaking the men's record by two hours!

In 1953, New Zealander Sir Edmund Hillary and Nepalese **Sherpa** Tenzing Norgay became the first people to climb to the highest point on Earth. They reached Mount Everest's 29,032-foot (8,849-meter) summit on May 29 after weeks of trekking. In 1954, Roger Bannister of England became the first person to run a mile in under four minutes.

These achievements proved that the impossible can be possible. Decades later, these athletes continue to inspire people around the world.

OLYMPICS OF THE 1950s

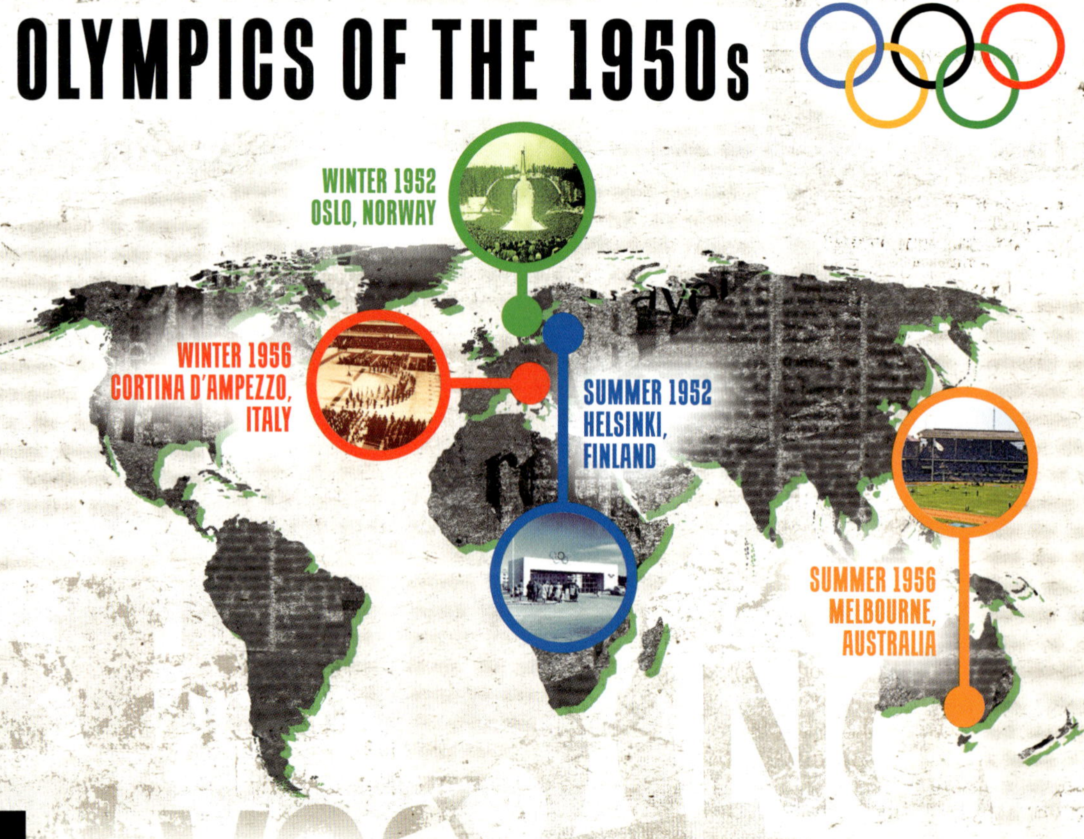

1952 SUMMER OLYMPICS

The 1952 Summer Olympics were held in Helsinki, Finland. The Soviet Union made its Olympic debut and sparked a fierce rivalry with the U.S., particularly in women's gymnastics. The standout athlete of the Games was runner Emil Zátopek from Czechoslovakia. He won three gold medals. His unique running style earned him the nickname "The Locomotive."

GORDIE HOWE

Gordie Howe was a Canadian professional ice hockey player. From 1946 to 1980, he played 26 seasons in the National Hockey League (NHL). During the 1952–1953 season, Howe scored a career high of 49 goals and became the first NHL player to score 95 points. He led the Detroit Red Wings to four Stanley Cup championships in the 1950s.

Gordie Howe

1956 WINTER OLYMPICS

The 1956 Winter Olympics were held in Cortina d'Ampezzo, Italy. Athletes represented 32 nations. This was the highest number of countries to take part in the Winter Olympics up to this point. The Soviet Union made its Winter Olympics debut and quickly became a dominant force, especially in ice hockey. It won more medals than any other country, including seven gold medals.

1956 SUMMER OLYMPICS

The 1956 Summer Olympics were held in Melbourne, Australia. However, major world events drove some countries to boycott the Games. Egypt, Iraq, Cambodia, and Lebanon opted out due to the Suez Canal crisis. The Netherlands, Switzerland, Liechtenstein, and Spain were protesting the Soviet invasion of Hungary. The People's Republic of China refused to participate because Taiwan had been allowed to compete.

PELÉ

Brazilian Pelé rose to fame as one of the world's top soccer players in 1958 after Brazil's national team won the World Cup. Pelé was born Edson Arantes do Nascimento in 1940 in Brazil. He began his professional career at age 15. At age 17, he became the youngest player to score a goal in a World Cup final.

TIMELINE

JANUARY 19, 1950
The Ladies' Professional Golf Association holds its inaugural tournament

MARCH 2, 1951
The first NBA All-Star Game is played in the Boston Garden

OCTOBER 2, 1950
Charles Schulz's first *Peanuts* cartoon strip is published in seven newspapers

FEBRUARY 6, 1952
Britain's Princess Elizabeth becomes Queen Elizabeth II after the death of her father, King George VI

FEBRUARY 27, 1951
The 22nd Amendment, which limits presidents to two terms in office, is ratified

APRIL 30, 1952
Mr. Potato Head is the first toy advertised on television

JUNE 25, 1950
The Korean War begins

JUNE 25, 1951
The first color commercial TV program airs on CBS

CBS

NOVEMBER 1, 1952
The U.S. drops the world's first hydrogen bomb at Enewetak Atoll in the Pacific Ocean

FEBRUARY 28, 1953
James Watson and Francis Crick announce the double-helix shape of DNA

MAY 17, 1954
The U.S. Supreme Court declares school segregation unconstitutional in the *Brown v. Board of Education* case

DECEMBER 23, 1954
20,000 Leagues Under the Sea comes out in theaters

1953
Dr. Jonas Salk develops the polio vaccine and tests it on himself and his family

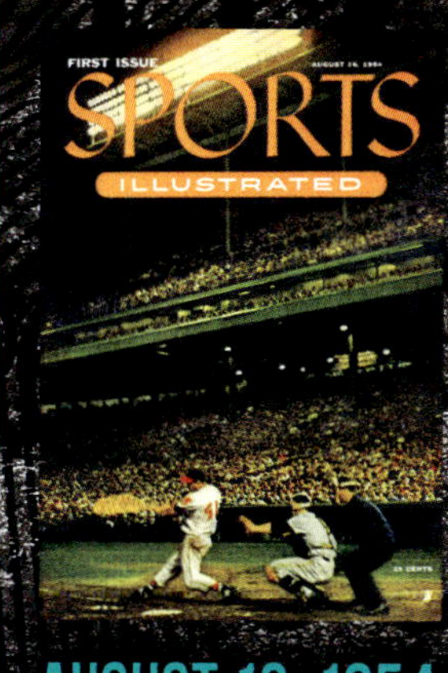

AUGUST 16, 1954
The first issue of *Sports Illustrated* is published

Edmund Hillary and Tenzing Norgay

MAY 29, 1953
Edmund Hillary and Tenzing Norgay become the first people to summit Mount Everest

MAY 14, 1955
The Warsaw Pact is formed to counter NATO

OCTOBER 29, 1956
The Suez Crisis begins in Egypt

MARCH 12, 1957
Dr. Seuss publishes *The Cat in the Hat*

DECEMBER 1, 1955
Rosa Parks refuses to give up her seat on a bus to a white man, an act that leads to the Montgomery Bus Boycott

JANUARY 28, 1956
Elvis Presley makes his first national television appearance on the CBS program *Stage Show*

SEPTEMBER 4, 1957
Attempts to desegregate a public school in Little Rock, Arkansas, cause great conflict

JULY 17, 1955
Disneyland opens in Anaheim, California

NOVEMBER 22 TO DECEMBER 8, 1956
A number of countries boycott the Summer Olympics in Melbourne, Australia

MARCH 27, 1958
Nikita Khrushchev becomes the Soviet premier

Barbie

MARCH 9, 1959
Barbie debuts at the American International Toy Fair in New York City

OCTOBER 4, 1957
The Soviet Union launches Sputnik 1, the world's first artificial satellite to orbit Earth

JANUARY 1, 1959
Fidel Castro becomes the leader of Cuba following a coup

JANUARY 28, 1958
The LEGO brick is launched

NATIONAL AERONAUTICS AND SPACE ADMINISTRATION U.S.A.

OCTOBER 1, 1958
NASA officially begins operations in the U.S.

1959
Alaska becomes a state on January 3 and Hawaii becomes a state on August 21

GLOSSARY

45s—phonograph records that spin at 45 revolutions per minute

angst—a feeling of deep anxiety or dread

antibiotics—medicines that prevent small, harmful organisms from growing

armistice—an agreement made by opposing sides in a war to temporarily stop fighting

assimilate—to be absorbed into the culture of a group

atomic weapons—devices that release nuclear energy to cause destruction

class-action lawsuit—a lawsuit brought by a few individuals on behalf of a much larger number who share the same interest in the outcome

Cold War—a conflict between the U.S. and the Soviet Union in the second half of the 1900s that did not break out into fighting

colonialism—the practice of extending and maintaining a nation's political and economic control over another people or area

communists—people who believe in communism; communism is a social system in which property and goods are controlled by the government.

discrimination—the act of treating someone unfairly because of race, gender, age, or other difference

DNA—a tiny substance that carries information about the makeup of a living thing

genetics—the study of how genes and traits are passed down from one generation to the next

genres—categories of a kind of art based on style, form, or content

Holocaust—the killing of millions of Jews and other people by the Nazis during World War II

LGBTQ+—a community of people who identify as something other than heterosexual or the gender they were assigned at birth; LGBTQ+ stands for Lesbian, Gay, Bisexual, Transgender, Queer and other identities.

nostalgia—a feeling of pleasure or sadness that is caused by remembering something from the past and wishing it could be experienced again

nuclear war—a conflict with nuclear weapons; nuclear weapons are extremely powerful and can produce destruction quickly with long-lasting effects.

redlining—the illegal practice of denying people access to loans, housing, and other services based on their race, ethnicity, or where they live

segregation—the act of separating people based on their race

Sherpa—a member of an ethnic group of people who live in the Himalayas and are often employed as guides or porters for mountain climbers

sock hop—a social event of the 1950s where teenagers danced in their socks to avoid damaging the floors of school gymnasiums or cafeterias

Soviet Union—short for the Union of Soviet Socialist Republics; the Soviet Union is a former country in Eastern Europe and western Asia made up of 15 republics or states that broke up in 1991.

stereophonic sound—a method of sound reproduction that creates a more realistic and immersive listening experience

synthesizers—musical instruments that have keyboards like a piano and can produce a wide variety of sounds

three-camera setup—a multi-camera production technique that uses three cameras to capture different angles of a scene

transistor—a small device that can switch electric currents on or off or amplify them

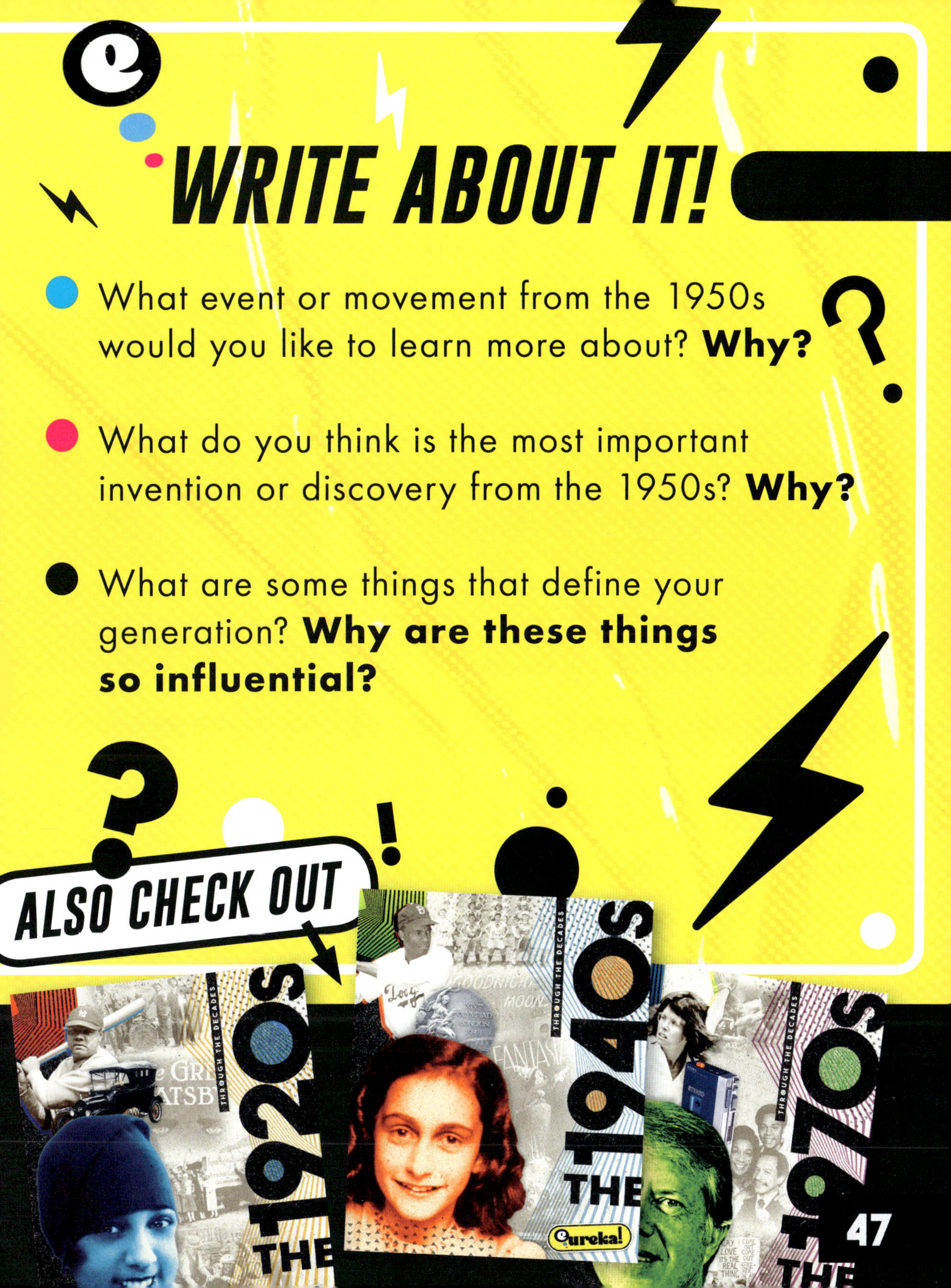

WRITE ABOUT IT!

- What event or movement from the 1950s would you like to learn more about? **Why?**

- What do you think is the most important invention or discovery from the 1950s? **Why?**

- What are some things that define your generation? **Why are these things so influential?**

ALSO CHECK OUT

INDEX

The images in this book are reproduced through the courtesy of: PictureLux/ The Hollywood Archive/ Alamy Stock Photo, front cover (Rosa Parks); INTERFOTO/ Alamy Stock Photo, front cover (radio); Everett Collection Inc/ Alamy Stock Photo, front cover (George Mikan), pp. 8 (hydrogen bomb), 21 (Boeing 707), 35 (Twenty-One); Alpha Historica/ Alamy Stock Photo, front cover (Martin Luther King Jr.); Wikimedia Commons/ Wikipedia, front cover (I Love Lucy), p. 14 (Warsaw Pact); Wikipedia/ Wikipedia, front cover (Charlotte's Web); ASSOCIATED PRESS/ AP Newsroom, front cover (NFL game); Allstar Picture Library Ltd/ Alamy Stock Photo, pp. 3 (Lady and the Tramp), 33 (Lady and the Tramp); Bill Waterson/ Alamy Stock Photo, pp. 3 (President Eisenhower), 10 (President Eisenhower); Michael Ochs Archives/ Stringer/ Getty Images, pp. 3 (Chuck Berry), 6, 37 (Chuck Berry, Elvis Presley); Science & Society Picture Library/ Contributor/ Getty Images, pp. 3 (H-bomb), 21 (H-bomb), 23 (heart-lung machine); Tim Gainey/ Alamy Stock Photo, p. 4 (Chevrolet); PixMix Images/ Alamy Stock Photo, p. 4 (45); Historic Collection/ Alamy Stock Photo, p. 4 (Bill Haley & His Comets); University of Southern California/ Contributor/ Getty Images, pp. 5 (sock hop), 8 (Disneyland); Camerique/ Contributor/ Getty Images, p. 5; Winai Tepsuttinun, p. 7 (gas); Artiom Photo, p. 7 (milk); Photo Builder, p. 7 (newspaper); phive2015, p. 7 (bread); AlenKadr, p. 7 (Coke); Bettmann/ Contributor/ Getty Images, pp. 8 (protest), 9 (sign), 11 (classroom), 13 (Thurgood Marshall), 15 (Suez Crisis), 19 (workforce), 23 (Watson and Crick), 24 (teenagers), 41 (Gordie Howe); Glasshouse Images/ Alamy Stock Photo, p. 9 (McCarthy); UniversalImagesGroup/ Contributor/ Getty Images, p. 9 (Rosa Parks); M&N/ Alamy Stock Photo, p. 11 (campaign); National Archives and Records Administration/ Wikipedia, p. 11 (signing); Carl Iwasaki/ Contributor/ Getty Images, p. 13 (Linda Brown); Phillip Harrington/ Alamy Stock Photo, p. 14 (Khrushchev); -/ Contributor/ Getty Images, pp. 14 (Moroccans), 22; Lois Herman/ Contributor/ Getty Images, p. 15 (Fidel Castro); jamesbenet/ Getty Images, p. 15 (Sputnik 1); ItzaVU, p. 16; MPI/ Stringer/ Getty Images, p. 17 (Douglas MacArthur); H. Armstrong Roberts/ ClassicStock/ Contributor/ Getty Images, pp. 18, 19 (baby boom), 29 (Hula Hoop); Harold M. Lambert/ Contributor/ Getty Images, pp. 19 (family), 27 (Ivy League); ClassicStock/ Contributor/ Getty Images, pp. 19 (suburbs), 29 (Mr. Potato Head); World History Archive/ Alamy Stock Photo, p. 20; Photo 12/ Contributor/ Getty Images, p. 23 (Rosalind Franklin); nobeastsofierce Science/ Alamy Stock Photo, p. 23 (polio); JoshBryan, p. 24 (Thunderbird); John Kobal Foundation/ Contributor/ Getty Images, p. 26; Anwar Hussein/ Alamy Stock Photo, p. 27 (bouffant); ClassicStock/ Alamy Stock Photo, p. 27 (poodle skirt); Archive Photos/ Stringer/ Getty Images, p. 27 (Elvis Presley); hris Willson/ Alamy Stock Photo, p. 28 (Matchbox Cars); dpa picture alliance/ Alamy Stock Photo, p. 28 (Barbie); Simon Robinson/ Easy On The Eye/ Alamy Stock Photo, p. 29 (LEGO); Morrow/ Wikipedia, p. 30 (Henry Huggins); Cover to Cover/ Alamy Stock Photo, p. 31 (Charlotte's Web); Pictorial Press Ltd/ Alamy Stock Photo, pp. 31 (Anne Frank), 35 (American Bandstand); Moviestore Collection Ltd/ Alamy Stock Photo, p. 32; PictureLux/ The Hollywood Archive/ Alamy Stock Photo, pp. 33 (20,000 Leagues Under the Sea), 34 (Father Knows Best); Allstar Picture Library Limited./ Alamy Stock Photo, p. 33 (Godzilla); PBH Images/ Alamy Stock Photo, p. 34 (Gunsmoke); imageBROKER.com/ Alamy Stock Photo, p. 34 (TV set); IanDagnall Computing/ Alamy Stock Photo, p. 35 (Lucille Ball); Nigel Osbourne/ Contributor/ Getty Images, p. 36; YAY Media AS/ Alamy Stock Photo, p. 37 (jukebox); Science History Images/ Alamy Stock Photo, p. 38 (Dick Button); Robert Riger/ Contributor/ Getty Images, p. 39 (NFL); PA Images/ Alamy Stock Photo, p. 39 (Althea Gibson); NTB/ Alamy Stock Photo, p. 40 (Norway, Italy); Chronicle/ Alamy Stock Photo, p. 40 (Finland); geogphotos/ Alamy Stock Photo, p. 40 (Australia); IBL/ Shutterstock, p. 41 (Pelé); United Kingdom Government/ Wikipedia, p. 42 (February, 1952); CBS Network/ Wikipedia, p. 42 (June, 1951); Keystone-France/ Contributor/ Getty Images, pp. 43 (November, 1952), 44 (May, 1955); Royal Geographical Society/ Contributor/ Getty Images, p. 43 (May, 1953); RLFE Pix/ Alamy Stock Photo, p. 43 (August, 1954); Anton Kravtcov/ Alamy Stock Vector, p. 44 (March, 1957); NASA Lewis/ Wikipedia, p. 45 (October, 1958); Chris Willson/ Alamy Stock Photo, p. 45 (March, 1959); Logopedia/ Wikipedia, p. 45 (logo, March, 1959).